92
ADD

CRF

Put Beginning Readers on the Right Track with
ALL ABOARD READING™

The All Aboard Reading series is especially designed for beginning readers. Written by noted authors and illustrated in full color, these are books that children really want to read—books to excite their imagination, expand their interests, make them laugh, and support their feelings. With fiction and nonfiction stories that are high interest and curriculum-related, All Aboard Reading books offer something for every young reader. And with four different reading levels, the All Aboard Reading series lets you choose which books are most appropriate for your children and their growing abilities.

Picture Readers
Picture Readers have super-simple texts, with many nouns appearing as rebus pictures. At the end of each book are 24 flash cards—on one side is a rebus picture; on the other side is the written-out word.

Station Stop 1
Station Stop 1 books are best for children who have just begun to read. Simple words and big type make these early reading experiences more comfortable. Picture clues help children to figure out the words on the page. Lots of repetition throughout the text helps children to predict the next word or phrase—an essential step in developing word recognition.

Station Stop 2
Station Stop 2 books are written specifically for children who are reading with help. Short sentences make it easier for early readers to understand what they are reading. Simple plots and simple dialogue help children with reading comprehension.

Station Stop 3
Station Stop 3 books are perfect for children who are reading alone. With longer text and harder words, these books appeal to children who have mastered basic reading skills. More complex stories captivate children who are ready for more challenging books.

In addition to All Aboard Reading books, look for All Aboard Math Readers™ (fiction stories that teach math concepts children are learning in school) and All Aboard Science Readers™ (nonfiction books that explore the most fascinating science topics in age-appropriate language).

All Aboard for happy reading!

For my wonderful nieces—
Megan, Sarah, and Anastasia
—P.D.

For my mother and Morgan
—M.M.

Library of Congress Cataloging-in-Publication Data

Demuth, Patricia.
    Johnny Appleseed / by Patricia Demuth ; illustrated by Michael Montgomery.
       p.   cm. — (All aboard reading. Level 1)
    Summary: Recounts the story of the man who traveled west planting apple seeds to make
the country a better place to live.
    1. Appleseed, Johnny, 1774–1845—Juvenile literature.   2. Apple growers—United
States—Biography—Juvenile literature.   3. Frontier and pioneer life—Middle West—
Juvenile literature.   [1. Appleseed, Johnny, 1774–1845.   2. Apple growers.   3. Frontier
and pioneer life.]   I. Montgomery, Michael, 1952-   .   II. Title.   III. Series.
    SB63.C46D45   1996
    634'.11'092—dc20   96-4015
    [B]   CIP
                                                                                                                  AC

ISBN 0-448-41130-X   2004 Printing

ALL ABOARD READING™

Station Stop 1

Johnny Appleseed

By Patricia Demuth
Illustrated by Michael Montgomery

Grosset & Dunlap • New York

Who was Johnny Appleseed?

Was he just in stories?

No.

Johnny was a real person.

His name was John Chapman.

He planted apple trees—

lots and lots of them.

So people called him

Johnny Appleseed.

Johnny was young
when our country was young.
Back then many people
were moving West.

There were no towns,
no schools,
not even many houses.
And there were no apple trees.
None at all.

Johnny was going West, too.
He wanted to plant apple trees.
He wanted to make the West
a nicer place to live.
So Johnny got a big, big bag.
He filled it with apple seeds.

Then he set out.

Johnny walked for days
and weeks.

On and on.

Soon his clothes were rags.

His feet were bare.

And what kind of hat
did he wear?

A cooking pot!

That way he didn't
have to carry it.

11

Snow came.

Did Johnny stop?

No.

He made snowshoes.
Then he walked
some more.

13

Spring came.

Johnny was out West now.

He stopped by a river.

He dug a hole.

Inside he put an apple seed.

Then he covered it with dirt.

Someday an apple tree
would stand here.
Johnny set out again.
He had lots more
seeds to plant.

Johnny walked by himself.

But he was not alone.

The animals were his friends.

Most people were afraid
of wild animals.
They had guns to shoot them.
But not Johnny.
One day a big, black bear
saw Johnny go by.
It did not hurt Johnny.
Maybe the bear knew
Johnny was a friend.

The Indians were
Johnny's friends, too.

They showed him how to find
good food—
berries and plants and roots.

Where did Johnny sleep?

Under the stars.

Johnny liked to lie on his back

and look up.

The wind blew softly.

Owls hooted.

The stars winked down at him.

Many years passed.
Johnny planted apple trees
everywhere.
People started to call him
Johnny Appleseed.

One day he came back to where
he had planted the first seed.
It was a big tree now.
A girl was swinging in it.

That night Johnny stayed
with the girl's family.
He told stories.
Everybody liked Johnny.
"Stay with us," they said.
"Make a home here."

But Johnny did not stay.
"I have work to do,"
he said.
"I am happy.
The whole world
is my home."

More and more people

came out West.

Johnny planted

more and more trees.

In the spring, the trees bloomed

with white flowers.

In the fall,
there were apples—
red, round, ripe apples.

People made apple pies.

And apple butter for their bread.

And apple cider to drink.
And children had apple trees
to climb.

It was all thanks
to Johnny Appleseed.